Protein Breakfasts Made Easy

Delicious Recipes for a Strong Start

Introduction

Starting your day with a high-protein breakfast can give you the energy and focus you need to power through the day. High-protein breakfasts not only keep you fuller for longer, but they also help build and maintain lean muscle mass, regulate blood sugar levels, and improve overall health.

If you're looking for inspiration to up your breakfast game and add more protein to your morning routine, this cookbook is for you. From delicious egg dishes and protein-packed smoothies to savory breakfast bowls and more, this cookbook features 50+ mouthwatering recipes that are easy to make and will fuel your day. Whether you're an athlete, a busy professional, or just looking to eat healthier, these high-protein breakfasts will help you start your day right and reach your nutrition goals.

Table of contents

High-Protein Breakfast Egg Muffins with Spinach, Feta, and Turkey Bacon

Ingredients:

- 4 large eggs
- 1/4 cup milk
- 1/4 teaspoon salt
- 1/4 teaspoon black pepper
- 1/2 cup chopped spinach
- 1/4 cup crumbled feta cheese
- 2 slices turkey bacon, cooked and crumbled

Instructions:

1. Preheat the oven to 350°F (175°C). Grease a muffin tin with cooking spray.
2. In a large bowl, whisk together the eggs, milk, salt, and black pepper.
3. Add the chopped spinach, crumbled feta cheese, and crumbled turkey bacon to the egg mixture. Stir to combine.
4. Pour the egg mixture evenly into the muffin cups, filling each about 3/4 full.
5. Bake for 20-25 minutes, or until the egg muffins are set and lightly golden on top.
6. Remove from the oven and let cool for a few minutes before removing the egg muffins from the muffin tin.
7. Serve warm and enjoy!

Cooking Time: 20-25 minutes

Calories per serve (2 people): 220 calories

Protein-Packed Greek Yogurt Bowl with Berries, Nuts, and Honey

Ingredients:

- 1 cup plain Greek yogurt
- 1/2 cup mixed berries (such as strawberries, blueberries, and raspberries)
- 1/4 cup chopped nuts (such as almonds, walnuts, or pecans)
- 1 tablespoon honey

Instructions:

1. Divide the Greek yogurt evenly between two bowls.
2. Top each bowl with half of the mixed berries and chopped nuts.
3. Drizzle 1/2 tablespoon of honey over each bowl.
4. Serve immediately.

Cooking Time: 5 minutes

Calories per serve (2 people): 250

High-Protein Breakfast Smoothie with Peanut Butter, Banana, and Chocolate Protein Powder

Ingredients:

- 1 banana
- 2 tablespoons peanut butter
- 1 scoop chocolate protein powder
- 1 cup unsweetened almond milk
- 1/2 cup ice cubes

Instructions:

1. Peel the banana and place it in a blender.
2. Add the peanut butter, chocolate protein powder, almond milk, and ice cubes to the blender.
3. Blend all the ingredients until smooth and creamy.
4. Pour the smoothie into two glasses and serve immediately.

Cooking Time: 5 minutes

Calories per serve (2 people): 350

Protein-Packed Breakfast Quinoa Bowl with Egg, Avocado, and Salsa

Ingredients:

- 1/2 cup quinoa
- 1 cup water
- 2 eggs
- 1 avocado, sliced
- 1/2 cup salsa
- Salt and pepper, to taste

Instructions:

1. Rinse quinoa in a fine mesh strainer and add to a medium saucepan with water. Bring to a boil, then reduce heat to low and cover. Cook for 15-20 minutes, or until water is absorbed and quinoa is tender.
2. While quinoa is cooking, fry eggs in a non-stick skillet over medium heat until cooked to your liking.
3. Divide cooked quinoa between two bowls. Top each bowl with a fried egg, sliced avocado, and salsa. Season with salt and pepper, to taste.
4. Serve immediately.

Cooking Time: 20 minutes

Calories per serve (2 people): 450

High-Protein Breakfast Burrito with Scrambled Eggs, Black Beans, and Cheese

Ingredients:

- 4 large eggs
- 1/2 cup canned black beans, drained and rinsed
- 1/4 cup shredded cheddar cheese
- 2 whole wheat tortillas
- 1 tablespoon olive oil
- Salt and pepper to taste

Instructions:

1. Crack the eggs into a bowl and whisk until well beaten. Season with salt and pepper to taste.
2. Heat the olive oil in a non-stick skillet over medium heat. Add the beaten eggs and cook, stirring occasionally, until scrambled and cooked through, about 3-4 minutes.
3. Add the black beans to the skillet and stir to combine with the scrambled eggs. Cook for an additional 1-2 minutes until the beans are heated through.
4. Divide the scrambled egg and black bean mixture evenly between the two tortillas. Sprinkle the shredded cheese on top of the egg mixture.
5. Roll up the tortillas tightly, tucking in the ends as you go. Serve immediately.

Cooking Time: 15 minutes

Calories per serve (2 people): 450

Protein-Packed Overnight Oats with Chia Seeds, Almond Milk, and Berries

Ingredients:

- 1 cup rolled oats
- 2 tablespoons chia seeds
- 1 cup unsweetened almond milk
- 1/4 cup vanilla protein powder
- 1/2 cup mixed berries
- 1 tablespoon honey (optional)

Instructions:

1. In a medium bowl, combine the rolled oats, chia seeds, almond milk, and protein powder. Stir well to combine.
2. Divide the mixture evenly between two jars or containers with lids.
3. Top each jar with mixed berries and drizzle with honey, if desired.
4. Cover the jars and refrigerate overnight.
5. In the morning, give the oats a stir and enjoy!

Cooking Time: Overnight

Calories per serve (2 people): 350

High-Protein Breakfast Sandwich with Canadian Bacon, Egg, and Cheese on Whole Grain English Muffin

Ingredients:

- 2 whole grain English muffins, split and toasted
- 4 slices of Canadian bacon
- 2 large eggs
- 2 slices of cheddar cheese
- Salt and pepper to taste

Instructions:

1. Preheat a non-stick skillet over medium heat.
2. Add the Canadian bacon slices to the skillet and cook for 2-3 minutes on each side until crispy. Remove from the skillet and set aside.
3. In the same skillet, crack the eggs and cook to your desired doneness. Season with salt and pepper to taste.
4. Place a slice of cheese on each English muffin half and toast in the oven or toaster oven until the cheese is melted and bubbly.
5. Assemble the sandwich by placing a slice of Canadian bacon on the bottom half of each English muffin. Top with a cooked egg and the other half of the English muffin.
6. Serve hot and enjoy!

Cooking Time: 10 minutes

Calories per serve (2 people): 400

Protein-Packed Breakfast Pancakes with Cottage Cheese and Berries

Ingredients:

- 1 cup of cottage cheese
- 2 eggs
- 1/2 cup of rolled oats
- 1/2 teaspoon of baking powder
- 1/2 teaspoon of vanilla extract
- 1/2 cup of mixed berries
- 1 tablespoon of honey

Instructions:

1. In a blender, combine the cottage cheese, eggs, rolled oats, baking powder, and vanilla extract. Blend until smooth.
2. Heat a non-stick pan over medium heat. Pour 1/4 cup of the batter onto the pan for each pancake.
3. Cook for 2-3 minutes on each side, or until golden brown.
4. Meanwhile, in a small saucepan, heat the mixed berries and honey over low heat until the berries are soft and the honey is melted.
5. Serve the pancakes with the warm berry sauce on top.

Cooking Time: 20 minutes

Calories per serve (2 people): 350

High-Protein Breakfast Frittata with Spinach, Mushrooms, and Feta Cheese

Ingredients:

- 4 large eggs
- 1/4 cup milk
- 1/4 teaspoon salt
- 1/4 teaspoon black pepper
- 1 tablespoon olive oil
- 1/2 cup sliced mushrooms
- 2 cups fresh spinach
- 1/4 cup crumbled feta cheese

Instructions:

1. Preheat the oven to 375°F (190°C).
2. In a medium bowl, whisk together the eggs, milk, salt, and black pepper.
3. Heat the olive oil in a 10-inch oven-safe skillet over medium heat.
4. Add the mushrooms and cook for 3-4 minutes, until they are tender.
5. Add the spinach and cook for 1-2 minutes, until it is wilted.
6. Pour the egg mixture into the skillet and stir to combine with the vegetables.
7. Sprinkle the feta cheese over the top of the egg mixture.
8. Transfer the skillet to the preheated oven and bake for 12-15 minutes, until the eggs are set and the cheese is melted and golden brown.
9. Remove the skillet from the oven and let it cool for a few minutes before slicing and serving.

Cooking Time: 25 minutes

Calories per serve (2 people): 350

Protein-Packed Breakfast Wrap with Turkey Sausage, Egg Whites, and Cheese

Ingredients:

- 4 turkey sausage links
- 4 egg whites
- 2 whole wheat tortillas
- 2 slices of low-fat cheese
- Salt and pepper to taste

Instructions:

1. Heat a non-stick skillet over medium heat. Add the turkey sausage links and cook for 5-7 minutes, or until browned and cooked through. Remove from skillet and set aside.
2. In the same skillet, add the egg whites and season with salt and pepper. Cook for 2-3 minutes, or until set. Remove from skillet and set aside.
3. Place the tortillas on a microwave-safe plate and heat in the microwave for 10-15 seconds, or until warm.
4. Place a slice of cheese on each tortilla. Divide the turkey sausage and egg whites evenly between the two tortillas.
5. Roll up the tortillas, tucking in the sides as you go. Serve immediately.

Cooking Time: 15 minutes

Calories per serve (2 people): 350

High-Protein Breakfast Skillet with Sweet Potato, Eggs, and Turkey Sausage

Ingredients:

- 1 large sweet potato, peeled and diced
- 4 turkey sausage links, sliced
- 1 red bell pepper, diced
- 1 yellow onion, diced
- 4 eggs
- 1 tablespoon olive oil
- Salt and pepper to taste

Instructions:

1. Heat the olive oil in a large skillet over medium-high heat.
2. Add the sweet potato and cook for 5-7 minutes, stirring occasionally, until it starts to soften.
3. Add the turkey sausage, red bell pepper, and onion to the skillet and cook for another 5-7 minutes, until the vegetables are tender and the sausage is browned.
4. Crack the eggs into the skillet and stir gently to combine with the other ingredients.
5. Cover the skillet and cook for 3-5 minutes, until the eggs are set to your liking.
6. Season with salt and pepper to taste.
7. Divide the skillet into two servings and enjoy!

Cooking Time: 25 minutes

Calories per serve (2 people): 450

Protein-Packed Breakfast Smoothie Bowl with Greek Yogurt, Almond Butter, and Fruit

Ingredients:

- 1 cup plain Greek yogurt
- 2 tablespoons almond butter
- 1 banana, sliced
- 1/2 cup frozen mixed berries
- 1/4 cup unsweetened almond milk
- 1 tablespoon honey
- 1/4 cup granola

Instructions:

1. In a blender, combine the Greek yogurt, almond butter, banana, mixed berries, almond milk, and honey. Blend until smooth.
2. Divide the smoothie mixture between two bowls.
3. Top each bowl with 2 tablespoons of granola.
4. Serve immediately.

Cooking Time: 5 minutes

Calories per serve (2 people): 350

High-Protein Breakfast Quiche with Ham, Broccoli, and Cheese

Ingredients:

- 1 pie crust
- 1 cup diced ham
- 1 cup chopped broccoli
- 1/2 cup shredded cheddar cheese
- 4 eggs
- 1/2 cup milk
- 1/4 teaspoon salt
- 1/4 teaspoon black pepper

Instructions:

1. Preheat the oven to 375°F (190°C).
2. Place the pie crust in a 9-inch pie dish and trim the edges.
3. Sprinkle the ham, broccoli, and cheese evenly over the bottom of the pie crust.
4. In a medium bowl, whisk together the eggs, milk, salt, and black pepper.
5. Pour the egg mixture over the ham, broccoli, and cheese in the pie crust.
6. Bake for 35-40 minutes, or until the quiche is set and the crust is golden brown.
7. Let the quiche cool for a few minutes before slicing and serving.

Cooking Time: 45 minutes

Calories per serve (2 people): 400

Protein-Packed Breakfast Parfait with Greek Yogurt, Berries, and Granola

Ingredients,:

- 1 cup Greek yogurt
- 1/2 cup mixed berries (such as strawberries, blueberries, and raspberries)
- 1/2 cup granola
- 1 tablespoon honey

Instructions:

1. In a small bowl, mix together the Greek yogurt and honey.
2. In two serving glasses or jars, layer the yogurt mixture, mixed berries, and granola.
3. Repeat the layers until the glasses or jars are full.
4. Refrigerate for at least 30 minutes before serving.

Cooking Time: 30 minutes (including refrigeration time)

Calories per serve (2 people): 300

High-Protein Breakfast Veggie Omelette with Mushrooms, Spinach, and Cheese

Ingredients:

- 4 eggs
- 1/4 cup chopped mushrooms
- 1/4 cup chopped spinach
- 1/4 cup shredded cheese
- 1 tablespoon olive oil
- Salt and pepper to taste

Instructions:

1. Crack the eggs into a bowl and whisk them together.
2. Heat the olive oil in a non-stick skillet over medium heat.
3. Add the mushrooms and spinach to the skillet and sauté for 2-3 minutes until they are tender.
4. Pour the eggs into the skillet and let them cook for 1-2 minutes until the bottom is set.
5. Sprinkle the cheese over the eggs and use a spatula to fold the omelette in half.
6. Cook for another 1-2 minutes until the cheese is melted and the eggs are cooked through.
7. Season with salt and pepper to taste.
8. Slide the omelette onto a plate and serve hot.

Cooking Time: 15 minutes

Calories per serve (2 people): 350

Protein-Packed Breakfast Chia Seed Pudding with Almond Milk and Nuts

Ingredients:

- 1/2 cup chia seeds
- 2 cups unsweetened almond milk
- 1/4 cup honey
- 1 tsp vanilla extract
- 1/4 cup chopped nuts (almonds, walnuts, or pecans)

Instructions:

1. In a mixing bowl, combine chia seeds, almond milk, honey, and vanilla extract. Stir well to combine.
2. Let the mixture sit for 5 minutes, then stir again to prevent clumping.
3. Cover the bowl with plastic wrap and refrigerate for at least 2 hours or overnight.
4. When ready to serve, divide the chia seed pudding into two bowls.
5. Sprinkle chopped nuts on top of each bowl and serve.

Cooking Time: 10 minutes

Calories per serve (2 people): 350

High-Protein Breakfast Bowl with Tofu Scramble, Avocado, and Whole Grain Toast

Ingredients:

- 1 block of firm tofu
- 1 tablespoon olive oil
- 1/2 teaspoon turmeric
- 1/2 teaspoon garlic powder
- 1/4 teaspoon salt
- 1 avocado, sliced
- 2 slices of whole grain toast
- Optional toppings: chopped fresh herbs, hot sauce, nutritional yeast

Instructions:

1. Drain the tofu and pat it dry with paper towels. Crumble the tofu into small pieces.
2. Heat the olive oil in a non-stick skillet over medium heat.
3. Add the crumbled tofu to the skillet and sprinkle with turmeric, garlic powder, and salt.
4. Cook the tofu, stirring occasionally, for 5-7 minutes or until it is heated through and slightly browned.
5. Toast the whole grain bread slices.
6. Divide the tofu scramble between two bowls.
7. Top each bowl with sliced avocado.
8. Serve with the whole grain toast on the side.
9. Add optional toppings, if desired.

Cooking Time: 15 minutes

Calories per serve (2 people): 400

Protein-Packed Breakfast Baked Oatmeal with Nuts, Fruit, and Greek Yogurt

Ingredients:

- 1 cup rolled oats
- 1/4 cup chopped nuts (such as almonds, pecans, or walnuts)
- 1/4 cup dried fruit (such as raisins, cranberries, or chopped dates)
- 1/2 teaspoon baking powder
- 1/2 teaspoon cinnamon
- 1/4 teaspoon salt
- 1 cup milk
- 1/4 cup plain Greek yogurt
- 1 egg
- 1 tablespoon honey
- 1/2 teaspoon vanilla extract

Instructions:

1. Preheat the oven to 375°F (190°C). Grease a 9-inch (23 cm) baking dish.
2. In a medium bowl, mix together the oats, nuts, dried fruit, baking powder, cinnamon, and salt.
3. In another bowl, whisk together the milk, Greek yogurt, egg, honey, and vanilla extract.
4. Pour the wet ingredients into the dry ingredients and stir until well combined.
5. Pour the mixture into the prepared baking dish and smooth out the top.
6. Bake for 25-30 minutes, or until the top is golden brown and the oatmeal is set.
7. Let cool for a few minutes before serving. Serve with additional Greek yogurt and fruit, if desired.

Cooking Time: 25-30 minutes

Calories per serve (2 people): 350

High-Protein Breakfast Stuffed Peppers with Turkey Sausage, Egg, and Cheese

Ingredients:

- 2 large bell peppers
- 4 turkey sausage links, casings removed
- 4 eggs
- 1/2 cup shredded cheddar cheese
- 1/4 cup chopped onion
- 1/4 cup chopped mushrooms
- 1/4 cup chopped spinach
- 1 tablespoon olive oil
- Salt and pepper to taste

Instructions:

1. Preheat oven to 375°F.
2. Cut off the tops of the bell peppers and remove the seeds and membranes.
3. In a skillet, heat olive oil over medium heat. Add onion and mushrooms and cook until softened, about 5 minutes.
4. Add turkey sausage to the skillet and cook until browned, breaking it up into small pieces with a spatula.
5. Add spinach to the skillet and cook until wilted, about 2 minutes.
6. Divide the sausage mixture evenly among the bell peppers.
7. Crack an egg into each bell pepper on top of the sausage mixture.
8. Sprinkle shredded cheese on top of each egg.
9. Season with salt and pepper to taste.
10. Bake in the preheated oven for 20-25 minutes or until the egg whites are set and the yolks are cooked to your liking.
11. Serve hot and enjoy!

Cooking Time: 30 minutes

Calories per serve (2 people): 350

Protein-Packed Breakfast Hash with Sweet Potato, Chicken Sausage, and Eggs

Ingredients:

- 1 large sweet potato, peeled and diced
- 2 chicken sausages, sliced
- 1 red bell pepper, diced
- 1/2 onion, diced
- 2 cloves garlic, minced
- 1 tsp paprika
- 1/2 tsp cumin
- 1/4 tsp salt
- 1/4 tsp black pepper
- 2 eggs
- 1 tbsp olive oil

Instructions:

1. Heat olive oil in a large skillet over medium heat.
2. Add sweet potato and cook for 5-7 minutes, stirring occasionally, until slightly softened.
3. Add chicken sausage, red bell pepper, onion, and garlic to the skillet. Cook for another 5-7 minutes, stirring occasionally, until vegetables are tender and sausage is browned.
4. Add paprika, cumin, salt, and black pepper to the skillet. Stir to combine.
5. Make two wells in the hash and crack an egg into each well.
6. Cover the skillet and cook for 5-7 minutes, or until the eggs are cooked to your liking.
7. Divide the hash into two plates and serve immediately.

Cooking Time: 30 minutes

Calories per serve (2 people): 450

High-Protein Breakfast Wrap with Scrambled Eggs, Turkey Bacon, and Cheese

Ingredients:

- 4 large eggs
- 4 slices of turkey bacon
- 2 whole wheat tortillas
- 1/4 cup shredded cheddar cheese
- 1 tablespoon olive oil
- Salt and pepper to taste

Instructions:

1. Crack the eggs into a bowl and whisk them together with salt and pepper.
2. Heat the olive oil in a non-stick skillet over medium heat.
3. Add the eggs to the skillet and scramble them until they are cooked through.
4. Cook the turkey bacon in a separate skillet until crispy.
5. Warm the tortillas in the microwave for 10-15 seconds.
6. Divide the scrambled eggs and turkey bacon between the two tortillas.
7. Sprinkle the shredded cheddar cheese on top of the eggs and bacon.
8. Roll up the tortillas and serve immediately.

Cooking Time: 15 minutes

Calories per serve (2 people): 450

Protein-Packed Breakfast Toast with Peanut Butter, Banana, and Chia Seeds

Ingredients:

- 2 slices of whole wheat bread
- 2 tablespoons of natural peanut butter
- 1 banana, sliced
- 1 tablespoon of chia seeds
- Optional: honey or maple syrup for drizzling

Instructions:

1. Toast the slices of bread until golden brown.
2. Spread 1 tablespoon of peanut butter on each slice of toast.
3. Arrange the sliced banana on top of the peanut butter.
4. Sprinkle 1/2 tablespoon of chia seeds on each slice of toast.
5. Optional: drizzle honey or maple syrup on top for added sweetness.
6. Serve immediately.

Cooking Time: 5 minutes

Calories per serve (2 people): 350 calories

High-Protein Breakfast Smoothie with Spinach, Greek Yogurt, and Protein Powder

Ingredients:

- 1 cup fresh spinach leaves
- 1 cup unsweetened almond milk
- 1/2 cup plain Greek yogurt
- 1 scoop vanilla protein powder
- 1/2 banana
- 1/2 teaspoon honey (optional)

Instructions:

1. Add spinach and almond milk to a blender and blend until smooth.
2. Add Greek yogurt, protein powder, banana, and honey (if using) to the blender and blend until smooth.
3. Pour the smoothie into two glasses and serve immediately.

Cooking Time: 5 minutes

Calories per serve (2 people): 200 calories

Protein-Packed Breakfast Shakshuka with Eggs, Tomatoes, and Chickpeas

Ingredients:

- 1 tablespoon olive oil
- 1 onion, chopped
- 2 garlic cloves, minced
- 1 red bell pepper, chopped
- 1 teaspoon ground cumin
- 1 teaspoon smoked paprika
- 1/4 teaspoon cayenne pepper
- 1 can (14.5 ounces) diced tomatoes
- 1 can (15 ounces) chickpeas, drained and rinsed
- 4 large eggs
- Salt and pepper, to taste
- 2 tablespoons chopped fresh parsley

Instructions:

1. Heat the olive oil in a large skillet over medium heat. Add the onion and garlic and cook until softened, about 5 minutes.
2. Add the red bell pepper, cumin, smoked paprika, and cayenne pepper. Cook for another 5 minutes.
3. Add the diced tomatoes and chickpeas and bring to a simmer. Cook for 10 minutes, stirring occasionally.
4. Make 4 wells in the tomato mixture and crack an egg into each well. Season with salt and pepper.
5. Cover the skillet and cook until the eggs are set, about 5-7 minutes.
6. Sprinkle with chopped parsley and serve hot.

Cooking Time: 30 minutes

Calories per serve (2 people): 400 calories

High-Protein Breakfast Sandwich with Grilled Chicken Breast, Avocado, and Cheese

Ingredients:

- 2 boneless, skinless chicken breasts
- 1 avocado, sliced
- 4 slices of cheese (cheddar or pepper jack)
- 4 slices of whole wheat bread
- 2 tablespoons olive oil
- Salt and pepper to taste

Instructions:

1. Preheat a grill or grill pan to medium-high heat.
2. Season the chicken breasts with salt and pepper on both sides.
3. Brush the chicken breasts with olive oil and place them on the grill.
4. Grill the chicken for 6-8 minutes on each side, or until cooked through.
5. While the chicken is cooking, toast the bread slices in a toaster or on a griddle.
6. When the chicken is done, remove it from the grill and let it rest for a few minutes.
7. Assemble the sandwiches by placing a slice of cheese on each slice of bread.
8. Top each slice of cheese with sliced avocado.
9. Slice the chicken breasts and place them on top of the avocado.
10. Top the sandwiches with the remaining slices of bread.
11. Cut the sandwiches in half and serve immediately.

Cooking Time: 20 minutes

Calories per serve (2 people): 550 calories

Protein-Packed Breakfast Power Bowl with Quinoa, Chicken Sausage, and Vegetables

Ingredients:

- 1 cup quinoa
- 2 cups water
- 2 chicken sausages, sliced
- 1 red bell pepper, diced
- 1 zucchini, diced
- 1/2 onion, diced
- 2 cloves garlic, minced
- 2 tablespoons olive oil
- Salt and pepper to taste
- 2 eggs, cooked to your liking

Instructions:

1. Rinse quinoa in a fine mesh strainer and add to a medium saucepan with 2 cups of water. Bring to a boil, then reduce heat to low and cover. Cook for 15-20 minutes or until all the water is absorbed and the quinoa is tender.
2. While the quinoa is cooking, heat 1 tablespoon of olive oil in a large skillet over medium-high heat. Add the chicken sausage and cook until browned, about 5 minutes. Remove from skillet and set aside.
3. Add the remaining tablespoon of olive oil to the skillet and add the red bell pepper, zucchini, onion, and garlic. Cook until the vegetables are tender, about 8-10 minutes.
4. Once the quinoa is done, fluff with a fork and divide between two bowls. Top each bowl with the cooked vegetables and chicken sausage.
5. Cook two eggs to your liking and place one on top of each bowl. Season with salt and pepper to taste.
6. Serve and enjoy!

Cooking Time: 30 minutes

Calories per serve (2 people): 550

High-Protein Breakfast Skillet with Ground Turkey, Sweet Potatoes, and Eggs

Ingredients:

- 1 tablespoon olive oil
- 1/2 pound ground turkey
- 1 medium sweet potato, peeled and diced
- 1/2 teaspoon garlic powder
- 1/2 teaspoon onion powder
- 1/2 teaspoon paprika
- 1/4 teaspoon salt
- 1/4 teaspoon black pepper
- 4 large eggs

Instructions:

1. Heat the olive oil in a large skillet over medium-high heat.
2. Add the ground turkey and cook until browned, breaking it up into small pieces as it cooks.
3. Add the sweet potato, garlic powder, onion powder, paprika, salt, and black pepper to the skillet. Stir to combine.
4. Cover the skillet and cook for 10-12 minutes, stirring occasionally, until the sweet potato is tender.
5. Make 4 wells in the sweet potato mixture and crack an egg into each well.
6. Cover the skillet and cook for an additional 5-7 minutes, or until the eggs are cooked to your liking.
7. Divide the skillet into 2 servings and serve immediately.

Cooking Time: 25-30 minutes

Calories per serve (2 people): 375 calories

Protein-Packed Breakfast Muffins with Ham, Cheese, and Vegetables

Ingredients:

- 6 eggs
- 1/4 cup milk
- 1/2 cup diced ham
- 1/2 cup shredded cheddar cheese
- 1/4 cup diced red bell pepper
- 1/4 cup diced green onion
- 1/4 teaspoon salt
- 1/4 teaspoon black pepper

Instructions:

1. Preheat the oven to 375°F (190°C). Grease a muffin tin with cooking spray.
2. In a large bowl, whisk together the eggs and milk until well combined.
3. Add the ham, cheese, red bell pepper, green onion, salt, and black pepper to the bowl. Stir to combine.
4. Divide the mixture evenly among the muffin cups.
5. Bake for 20-25 minutes, or until the muffins are set and lightly golden on top.
6. Remove from the oven and let cool for a few minutes before serving.

Cooking Time: 25 minutes

Calories per serve (2 people): 350

High-Protein Breakfast Scramble with Tofu, Vegetables, and Whole Grain Toast

Ingredients:

- 1 block of firm tofu, drained and crumbled
- 1 tablespoon olive oil
- 1/2 onion, diced
- 1/2 red bell pepper, diced
- 1/2 green bell pepper, diced
- 1/2 teaspoon garlic powder
- 1/2 teaspoon turmeric
- Salt and pepper to taste
- 2 slices of whole grain bread, toasted

Instructions:

1. Heat the olive oil in a large skillet over medium heat.
2. Add the onion and bell peppers and sauté for 5 minutes, or until the vegetables are tender.
3. Add the crumbled tofu, garlic powder, turmeric, salt, and pepper to the skillet and stir to combine.
4. Cook for 5-7 minutes, or until the tofu is heated through and slightly browned.
5. Divide the scramble between two plates and serve with the toasted whole grain bread.

Cooking Time: 20 minutes

Calories per serve (2 people): 300 calories

Protein-Packed Breakfast Smoothie with Vanilla Greek Yogurt, Blueberries, and Almond Milk

Ingredients:

- 1 cup frozen blueberries
- 1 cup unsweetened almond milk
- 1/2 cup vanilla Greek yogurt
- 1 scoop vanilla protein powder
- 1 tablespoon honey

Instructions:

1. Add all ingredients to a blender.
2. Blend until smooth and creamy.
3. Pour into two glasses and serve immediately.

Cooking Time: 5 minutes

Calories per serve (2 people): 250

High-Protein Breakfast Stuffed Sweet Potatoes with Eggs, Turkey Sausage, and Cheese

Ingredients:

- 2 medium sweet potatoes
- 4 turkey sausage links, sliced
- 4 eggs
- 1/2 cup shredded cheddar cheese
- 1 tablespoon olive oil
- Salt and pepper to taste

Instructions:

1. Preheat the oven to 400°F (200°C).
2. Wash the sweet potatoes and prick them all over with a fork. Place them on a baking sheet and bake for 45-50 minutes, or until tender.
3. While the sweet potatoes are baking, heat the olive oil in a skillet over medium heat. Add the sliced turkey sausage and cook until browned, about 5-7 minutes.
4. Crack the eggs into the skillet with the turkey sausage and cook until the whites are set but the yolks are still runny, about 3-4 minutes.
5. Remove the sweet potatoes from the oven and let them cool for a few minutes. Cut them in half lengthwise and scoop out some of the flesh to make a well in each half.
6. Divide the turkey sausage and egg mixture between the four sweet potato halves. Top each half with shredded cheddar cheese.
7. Return the stuffed sweet potatoes to the oven and bake for an additional 5-7 minutes, or until the cheese is melted and bubbly.
8. Serve hot and enjoy!

Cooking Time: 1 hour

Calories per serve (2 people): 450

Protein-Packed Breakfast Frittata Muffins with Broccoli, Cheddar Cheese, and Egg Whites

Ingredients:

- 1 cup broccoli florets, chopped
- 1/2 cup shredded cheddar cheese
- 6 egg whites
- 2 whole eggs
- 1/4 cup milk
- 1/4 teaspoon salt
- 1/4 teaspoon black pepper
- Non-stick cooking spray

Instructions:

1. Preheat oven to 375°F (190°C).
2. Grease a muffin tin with non-stick cooking spray.
3. In a mixing bowl, whisk together the egg whites, whole eggs, milk, salt, and black pepper.
4. Add the chopped broccoli and shredded cheddar cheese to the mixing bowl and stir to combine.
5. Pour the mixture evenly into the muffin tin, filling each cup about 3/4 full.
6. Bake for 20-25 minutes, or until the frittata muffins are set and lightly golden on top.
7. Remove from the oven and let cool for a few minutes before serving.

Cooking Time: 20-25 minutes

Calories per serve (2 people): 220 calories

High-Protein Breakfast Smoothie with Greek Yogurt, Pineapple, and Coconut

Ingredients:

- 1 cup Greek yogurt
- 1 cup frozen pineapple chunks
- 1/2 cup unsweetened coconut milk
- 1/4 cup unsweetened shredded coconut
- 1 scoop vanilla protein powder
- 1/2 teaspoon vanilla extract
- 1/2 cup ice cubes

Instructions:

1. Add all ingredients to a blender.
2. Blend until smooth and creamy.
3. Pour into two glasses and serve immediately.

Cooking Time: 5 minutes

Calories per serve (2 people): 300

Protein-Packed Breakfast Tacos with Scrambled Eggs, Black Beans, and Avocado

Ingredients:

- 4 small corn tortillas
- 4 large eggs
- 1/2 cup canned black beans, drained and rinsed
- 1/2 avocado, sliced
- 1/4 cup shredded cheddar cheese
- 1 tablespoon olive oil
- Salt and pepper to taste

Instructions:

1. Heat the olive oil in a non-stick skillet over medium heat.
2. Add the black beans and cook for 2-3 minutes, stirring occasionally.
3. Crack the eggs into a bowl and whisk until well beaten. Add salt and pepper to taste.
4. Pour the eggs into the skillet with the black beans and cook, stirring occasionally, until the eggs are scrambled and cooked through.
5. Warm the tortillas in the microwave or on a skillet.
6. Divide the scrambled eggs and black beans among the tortillas.
7. Top each taco with sliced avocado and shredded cheddar cheese.
8. Serve immediately.

Cooking Time: 15 minutes

Calories per serve (2 people): 450

High-Protein Breakfast Bowl with Quinoa, Lentils, and Roasted Vegetables

Ingredients:

- 1/2 cup quinoa
- 1/2 cup lentils
- 1 red bell pepper, sliced
- 1 zucchini, sliced
- 1/2 red onion, sliced
- 2 tablespoons olive oil
- 1 teaspoon garlic powder
- 1 teaspoon paprika
- Salt and pepper, to taste
- 2 eggs

Instructions:

1. Preheat the oven to 400°F (200°C).
2. Cook the quinoa and lentils according to package instructions.
3. In a large bowl, toss the sliced bell pepper, zucchini, and red onion with olive oil, garlic powder, paprika, salt, and pepper.
4. Spread the vegetables in a single layer on a baking sheet and roast for 20-25 minutes, or until tender and slightly charred.
5. While the vegetables are roasting, fry the eggs in a non-stick pan over medium heat until cooked to your liking.
6. Divide the cooked quinoa and lentils between two bowls.
7. Top each bowl with half of the roasted vegetables and a fried egg.
8. Serve immediately.

Cooking Time: 30-35 minutes

Calories per serve (2 people): 450 calories

Protein-Packed Breakfast Bars with Oats, Nuts, and Protein Powder

Ingredients:

- 1 cup rolled oats
- 1/2 cup chopped nuts (almonds, pecans, or walnuts)
- 1/2 cup vanilla protein powder
- 1/4 cup honey
- 1/4 cup almond butter
- 1/4 cup unsweetened almond milk
- 1/4 cup dried cranberries or raisins

Instructions:

1. Preheat the oven to 350°F (180°C). Line an 8-inch square baking dish with parchment paper.
2. In a large bowl, mix together the oats, chopped nuts, and protein powder.
3. In a small saucepan, heat the honey, almond butter, and almond milk over low heat until melted and smooth.
4. Pour the honey mixture over the oat mixture and stir until well combined.
5. Stir in the dried cranberries or raisins.
6. Press the mixture into the prepared baking dish and smooth the top with a spatula.
7. Bake for 15-20 minutes, or until the edges are golden brown.
8. Let cool completely in the pan before cutting into bars.

Cooking Time: 15-20 minutes

Calories per serve (2 people): 350 calories

High-Protein Breakfast Salad with Hard-Boiled Eggs, Bacon, and Mixed Greens

Ingredients:

- 4 cups mixed greens
- 4 hard-boiled eggs, sliced
- 4 slices of bacon, cooked and crumbled
- 1/2 cup cherry tomatoes, halved
- 1/4 cup red onion, thinly sliced
- 1/4 cup crumbled feta cheese
- 2 tablespoons olive oil
- 1 tablespoon balsamic vinegar
- Salt and pepper to taste

Instructions:

1. In a large bowl, combine the mixed greens, sliced hard-boiled eggs, crumbled bacon, cherry tomatoes, red onion, and crumbled feta cheese.
2. In a small bowl, whisk together the olive oil, balsamic vinegar, salt, and pepper.
3. Pour the dressing over the salad and toss to combine.
4. Divide the salad between two plates and serve immediately.

Cooking Time: 20 minutes

Calories per serve (2 people): 400

Protein-Packed Breakfast Crepes with Cottage Cheese and Fresh Berries

Ingredients:

- 1/2 cup all-purpose flour
- 1/2 cup milk
- 2 eggs
- 1/4 teaspoon salt
- 1/2 cup cottage cheese
- 1/2 cup fresh berries (such as strawberries, blueberries, or raspberries)

Instructions:

1. In a medium bowl, whisk together the flour, milk, eggs, and salt until smooth.
2. Heat a nonstick skillet over medium heat. Pour 1/4 cup of the batter into the skillet and swirl to coat the bottom of the pan. Cook for 1-2 minutes, or until the edges start to lift away from the pan and the bottom is golden brown. Flip the crepe and cook for an additional 30 seconds to 1 minute, or until the other side is golden brown. Repeat with the remaining batter, making 4 crepes total.
3. Spread 2 tablespoons of cottage cheese onto each crepe. Top with fresh berries.
4. Roll up the crepes and serve immediately.

Cooking Time: 15 minutes

Calories per serve (2 people): 250

High-Protein Breakfast Quinoa Bowl with Grilled Chicken, Roasted Vegetables, and Hummus

Ingredients:

- 1 cup quinoa
- 2 cups water
- 2 chicken breasts
- 1 red bell pepper, sliced
- 1 zucchini, sliced
- 1 tablespoon olive oil
- 1/2 teaspoon salt
- 1/4 teaspoon black pepper
- 1/2 cup hummus
- 2 tablespoons chopped fresh parsley

Instructions:

1. Rinse the quinoa in a fine mesh strainer and add it to a medium saucepan with 2 cups of water. Bring to a boil, then reduce the heat to low and cover. Cook for 15-20 minutes, or until the water is absorbed and the quinoa is tender.
2. While the quinoa is cooking, preheat a grill or grill pan to medium-high heat. Season the chicken breasts with salt and pepper, then grill for 6-7 minutes per side, or until cooked through. Let the chicken rest for 5 minutes, then slice into strips.
3. Preheat the oven to 400°F. Toss the sliced bell pepper and zucchini with olive oil, salt, and pepper, then spread them out on a baking sheet. Roast for 15-20 minutes, or until tender and lightly browned.
4. To assemble the bowls, divide the cooked quinoa between two bowls. Top with the sliced chicken, roasted vegetables, and hummus. Sprinkle with chopped parsley and serve.

Cooking Time: 30 minutes

Calories per serve (2 people): 500

Protein-Packed Breakfast Cheddar Biscuits with Sausage and Egg

Ingredients:

- 1 cup all-purpose flour
- 1/2 teaspoon salt
- 1 tablespoon baking powder
- 1/4 cup unsalted butter, cold and cubed
- 1/2 cup shredded cheddar cheese
- 1/2 cup milk
- 2 sausage patties
- 2 eggs
- Salt and pepper to taste

Instructions:

1. Preheat the oven to 400°F (200°C).
2. In a large bowl, whisk together the flour, salt, and baking powder.
3. Add the cold butter and use a pastry cutter or your fingers to cut the butter into the flour mixture until it resembles coarse crumbs.
4. Stir in the shredded cheddar cheese and milk until just combined.
5. Turn the dough out onto a floured surface and knead gently until it comes together.
6. Roll the dough out to 1/2 inch thickness and use a biscuit cutter to cut out 4 biscuits.
7. Place the biscuits on a baking sheet lined with parchment paper and bake for 15-18 minutes or until golden brown.
8. While the biscuits are baking, cook the sausage patties in a skillet over medium heat until browned and cooked through.
9. Remove the sausage from the skillet and set aside.
10. In the same skillet, crack the eggs and cook to your desired doneness.
11. Season the eggs with salt and pepper to taste.
12. To assemble, split the biscuits in half and place a sausage patty and a cooked egg on each biscuit.
13. Serve immediately.

Cooking Time: 30 minutes

Calories per serve (2 people): 600

High-Protein Breakfast Burrito with Eggs, Black Beans, and Avocado

Ingredients:

- 4 large eggs
- 1/2 cup canned black beans, drained and rinsed
- 1/2 avocado, diced
- 2 whole wheat tortillas
- 1/4 cup shredded cheddar cheese
- 1 tablespoon olive oil
- Salt and pepper to taste

Instructions:

1. In a small bowl, whisk the eggs with salt and pepper.
2. Heat the olive oil in a non-stick skillet over medium heat.
3. Add the eggs and scramble until cooked through, about 3-4 minutes.
4. Add the black beans and stir to combine.
5. Warm the tortillas in the microwave for 10-15 seconds.
6. Divide the egg and bean mixture between the two tortillas.
7. Top each with diced avocado and shredded cheese.
8. Roll up the tortillas and serve immediately.

Cooking Time: 15 minutes

Calories per serve (2 people): 450

Protein-Packed Breakfast Omelet with Spinach, Mushrooms, and Feta Cheese

Ingredients:

- 4 large eggs
- 1/4 cup of milk
- 1/2 cup of fresh spinach, chopped
- 1/2 cup of mushrooms, sliced
- 1/4 cup of crumbled feta cheese
- 1 tablespoon of olive oil
- Salt and pepper to taste

Instructions:

1. In a bowl, whisk together the eggs and milk. Season with salt and pepper.
2. Heat the olive oil in a non-stick skillet over medium heat.
3. Add the mushrooms and cook for 2-3 minutes until they start to soften.
4. Add the spinach and cook for another 1-2 minutes until wilted.
5. Pour the egg mixture into the skillet and let it cook for 2-3 minutes until the edges start to set.
6. Sprinkle the feta cheese over the top of the omelet.
7. Using a spatula, fold the omelet in half and cook for another 1-2 minutes until the cheese is melted and the eggs are cooked through.
8. Slide the omelet onto a plate and serve hot.

Cooking Time: 15 minutes

Calories per serve (2 people): 350

High-Protein Breakfast Pancakes with Cottage Cheese and Blueberries

Ingredients:

- 1 cup rolled oats
- 1/2 cup low-fat cottage cheese
- 2 eggs
- 1/2 teaspoon baking powder
- 1/2 teaspoon vanilla extract
- 1/2 cup blueberries
- 1 tablespoon honey
- Non-stick cooking spray

Instructions:

1. In a blender, combine rolled oats, cottage cheese, eggs, baking powder, and vanilla extract. Blend until smooth.
2. Heat a non-stick skillet over medium heat. Spray with non-stick cooking spray.
3. Using a 1/4 cup measuring cup, pour batter onto the skillet. Cook until bubbles form on the surface of the pancake, then flip and cook for an additional 1-2 minutes.
4. Repeat with remaining batter.
5. In a small saucepan, heat blueberries and honey over medium heat until the blueberries burst and the mixture thickens slightly.
6. Serve pancakes topped with blueberry sauce.

Cooking Time: 15 minutes

Calories per serve (2 pancakes): 320

Protein-Packed Breakfast Yogurt Bowl with Granola, Almonds, and Berries

Ingredients:

- 1 cup plain Greek yogurt
- 1/2 cup granola
- 1/4 cup sliced almonds
- 1/2 cup mixed berries (such as strawberries, blueberries, and raspberries)
- 1 tablespoon honey

Instructions:

1. Divide the Greek yogurt evenly between two bowls.
2. Top each bowl with 1/4 cup of granola, 2 tablespoons of sliced almonds, and 1/4 cup of mixed berries.
3. Drizzle 1/2 tablespoon of honey over each bowl.
4. Serve immediately.

Cooking Time: 5 minutes

Calories per serve (2 people): 350

High-Protein Breakfast Stuffed Peppers with Eggs, Turkey Sausage, and Cheese

Ingredients:

- 2 large bell peppers, halved and seeded
- 4 eggs
- 4 turkey sausage links, cooked and chopped
- 1/2 cup shredded cheddar cheese
- 1/4 cup chopped onion
- 1/4 cup chopped red bell pepper
- 1/4 cup chopped green bell pepper
- 1 tablespoon olive oil
- Salt and pepper to taste

Instructions:

1. Preheat oven to 375°F (190°C).
2. Place the bell pepper halves in a baking dish and brush with olive oil. Bake for 10 minutes.
3. In a skillet, sauté the onion, red bell pepper, and green bell pepper until tender.
4. Add the chopped turkey sausage to the skillet and cook for 2-3 minutes.
5. Crack an egg into each bell pepper half. Season with salt and pepper.
6. Top each bell pepper half with the sautéed vegetables and turkey sausage.
7. Sprinkle shredded cheddar cheese over the top of each bell pepper half.
8. Bake for 15-20 minutes or until the eggs are cooked to your liking.
9. Serve hot and enjoy!

Cooking Time: 30 minutes

Calories per serve (2 people): 400

Protein-Packed Breakfast Energy Balls with Peanut Butter, Oats, and Chocolate Chips

Ingredients:

- 1 cup rolled oats
- 1/2 cup peanut butter
- 1/4 cup honey
- 1/4 cup chocolate chips
- 1/4 cup chia seeds
- 1/4 cup ground flaxseed

Instructions:

1. In a large mixing bowl, combine rolled oats, peanut butter, honey, chocolate chips, chia seeds, and ground flaxseed.
2. Mix all ingredients together until well combined.
3. Using your hands, form the mixture into small balls, about 1 inch in diameter.
4. Place the balls on a baking sheet lined with parchment paper.
5. Refrigerate the balls for at least 30 minutes to set.
6. Once set, the energy balls can be stored in an airtight container in the refrigerator for up to 1 week.

Cooking Time: 10 minutes

Calories per serve (2 people): 250

High-Protein Breakfast Bagel Sandwich with Smoked Salmon, Cream Cheese, and Arugula

Ingredients:

- 2 bagels, sliced in half
- 4 oz smoked salmon
- 4 tbsp cream cheese
- 1 cup arugula
- 1 tbsp olive oil
- Salt and pepper to taste

Instructions:

1. Preheat the oven to 350°F.
2. Place the bagel halves on a baking sheet and toast in the oven for 5 minutes.
3. In a small bowl, mix the cream cheese with salt and pepper to taste.
4. Spread the cream cheese mixture on each bagel half.
5. Top each bagel half with smoked salmon and arugula.
6. Drizzle with olive oil and season with salt and pepper to taste.
7. Serve and enjoy!

Cooking Time: 10 minutes

Calories per serve (2 people): 450

Protein-Packed Breakfast Quiche with Ham, Broccoli, and Swiss Cheese

Ingredients:

- 1 pie crust
- 1 cup diced ham
- 1 cup chopped broccoli
- 1 cup shredded Swiss cheese
- 4 eggs
- 1 cup milk
- 1/2 teaspoon salt
- 1/4 teaspoon black pepper

Instructions:

1. Preheat the oven to 375°F (190°C).
2. Place the pie crust in a 9-inch (23cm) pie dish and prick the bottom with a fork.
3. Sprinkle the ham, broccoli, and Swiss cheese over the pie crust.
4. In a mixing bowl, whisk together the eggs, milk, salt, and black pepper.
5. Pour the egg mixture over the ham, broccoli, and Swiss cheese.
6. Bake for 40-45 minutes, or until the quiche is set and the top is golden brown.
7. Let the quiche cool for a few minutes before slicing and serving.

Cooking Time: 45 minutes

Calories per serve (2 people): 400

High-Protein Breakfast Waffle with Greek Yogurt and Fresh Fruit

Ingredients:

- 1 cup of whole wheat flour
- 1 scoop of vanilla protein powder
- 1 teaspoon of baking powder
- 1/2 teaspoon of cinnamon
- 1/4 teaspoon of salt
- 1 egg
- 1 cup of unsweetened almond milk
- 1 tablespoon of honey
- 1/2 teaspoon of vanilla extract
- 1/2 cup of Greek yogurt
- 1 cup of fresh fruit (such as berries or sliced bananas)

Instructions:

1. In a large bowl, whisk together the flour, protein powder, baking powder, cinnamon, and salt.
2. In a separate bowl, beat the egg and then add the almond milk, honey, and vanilla extract. Mix well.
3. Pour the wet ingredients into the dry ingredients and stir until just combined.
4. Preheat your waffle iron and spray with cooking spray.
5. Spoon the batter onto the waffle iron and cook according to the manufacturer's instructions.
6. While the waffles are cooking, mix the Greek yogurt with a little honey or maple syrup to sweeten it.
7. Top the waffles with the Greek yogurt and fresh fruit.
8. Serve and enjoy!

Cooking Time: 15 minutes

Calories per serve (2 people): 400

Protein-Packed Breakfast Sausage and Egg Muffins with Spinach and Cheese

Ingredients:

- 4 eggs
- 1/2 cup cooked spinach
- 1/4 cup shredded cheddar cheese
- 4 breakfast sausage links, cooked and chopped
- 1/4 teaspoon salt
- 1/4 teaspoon black pepper

Instructions:

1. Preheat the oven to 350°F (175°C).
2. In a mixing bowl, whisk together the eggs, salt, and black pepper.
3. Add the cooked spinach, shredded cheddar cheese, and chopped breakfast sausage to the mixing bowl. Mix well.
4. Grease a muffin tin with cooking spray.
5. Pour the egg mixture evenly into the muffin cups.
6. Bake for 20-25 minutes or until the egg muffins are set and golden brown on top.
7. Remove from the oven and let cool for a few minutes before serving.

Cooking Time: 25 minutes

Calories per serve (2 people): 350

High-Protein Breakfast Baked Oatmeal with Peanut Butter, Banana, and Chocolate Chips

Ingredients:

- 2 cups rolled oats
- 1/4 cup peanut butter
- 1 ripe banana, mashed
- 1/4 cup honey
- 1/2 cup unsweetened almond milk
- 1 egg
- 1 tsp vanilla extract
- 1 tsp baking powder
- 1/4 tsp salt
- 1/4 cup chocolate chips

Instructions:

1. Preheat the oven to 350°F (180°C).
2. In a large mixing bowl, combine the rolled oats, peanut butter, mashed banana, honey, almond milk, egg, vanilla extract, baking powder, and salt. Mix well.
3. Stir in the chocolate chips.
4. Pour the mixture into a greased 8x8 inch baking dish.
5. Bake for 25-30 minutes, or until the top is golden brown and the oatmeal is set.
6. Let cool for a few minutes before serving.

Cooking Time: 30 minutes

Calories per serve (2 people): 450

Protein-Packed Breakfast Bowl with Roasted Sweet Potato, Chickpeas, and Poached Eggs

Ingredients:

- 1 large sweet potato, peeled and diced
- 1 can chickpeas, drained and rinsed
- 1 tablespoon olive oil
- 1 teaspoon smoked paprika
- 1/2 teaspoon garlic powder
- 1/2 teaspoon salt
- 4 large eggs
- 1 avocado, sliced
- 2 tablespoons chopped fresh cilantro

Instructions:

1. Preheat the oven to 400°F (200°C).
2. In a large bowl, toss the sweet potato and chickpeas with olive oil, smoked paprika, garlic powder, and salt.
3. Spread the sweet potato and chickpeas in a single layer on a baking sheet and roast for 20-25 minutes, or until tender and lightly browned.
4. While the sweet potato and chickpeas are roasting, poach the eggs. Fill a large saucepan with water and bring to a simmer. Crack each egg into a small bowl or ramekin. Using a spoon, create a whirlpool in the simmering water and gently pour the egg into the center of the whirlpool. Cook for 3-4 minutes, or until the whites are set and the yolks are still runny. Use a slotted spoon to remove the eggs from the water and place on a paper towel to drain.
5. Divide the sweet potato and chickpea mixture between two bowls. Top each bowl with two poached eggs, sliced avocado, and chopped cilantro.
6. Serve immediately.

Cooking Time: 30-35 minutes

Calories per serve (2 people): 450

High-Protein Breakfast Egg and Cheese Sandwich with Turkey Bacon and Spinach

Ingredients:

- 4 slices of turkey bacon
- 4 large eggs
- 2 slices of cheddar cheese
- 2 whole wheat English muffins
- 1 cup of fresh spinach leaves
- Salt and pepper to taste

Instructions:

1. Cook the turkey bacon in a non-stick skillet over medium heat until crispy. Remove from skillet and set aside.
2. In the same skillet, crack the eggs and cook until the whites are set and the yolks are still runny. Season with salt and pepper to taste.
3. Toast the English muffins until lightly browned.
4. Place a slice of cheese on each English muffin half.
5. Top each muffin half with a handful of fresh spinach leaves.
6. Place two slices of turkey bacon on top of the spinach.
7. Top each sandwich with a cooked egg.
8. Season with additional salt and pepper if desired.
9. Serve immediately and enjoy!

Cooking Time: 10 minutes

Calories per serve (2 people): 450

Protein-Packed Breakfast Turkey Sausage and Egg Scramble with Bell Peppers and Onions

Ingredients:

- 4 turkey sausage links, sliced
- 1/2 red bell pepper, diced
- 1/2 green bell pepper, diced
- 1/2 onion, diced
- 4 eggs
- 1/4 cup milk
- 1/4 cup shredded cheddar cheese
- Salt and pepper to taste
- 1 tablespoon olive oil

Instructions:

1. Heat olive oil in a large skillet over medium heat.
2. Add turkey sausage, bell peppers, and onion. Cook until sausage is browned and vegetables are tender, about 5-7 minutes.
3. In a bowl, whisk together eggs, milk, salt, and pepper.
4. Pour egg mixture into skillet with sausage and vegetables. Cook, stirring occasionally, until eggs are set, about 5-7 minutes.
5. Sprinkle shredded cheddar cheese over the top of the egg mixture and let it melt.
6. Divide the scramble into two plates and serve hot.

Cooking Time: 15 minutes

Calories per serve (2 people): 350

High-Protein Breakfast Cottage Cheese Pancakes with Blueberries and Honey

Ingredients:

- 1 cup low-fat cottage cheese
- 1/2 cup rolled oats
- 2 eggs
- 1/2 teaspoon vanilla extract
- 1/4 teaspoon cinnamon
- 1/2 cup blueberries
- 2 tablespoons honey

Instructions:

1. In a blender, combine cottage cheese, rolled oats, eggs, vanilla extract, and cinnamon. Blend until smooth.
2. Heat a non-stick skillet over medium heat. Pour 1/4 cup of the batter onto the skillet for each pancake.
3. Cook for 2-3 minutes on each side, or until golden brown.
4. Top each pancake with blueberries and drizzle with honey.
5. Serve immediately.

Cooking Time: 15 minutes

Calories per serve (2 pancakes): 320

Protein-Packed Breakfast Tofu Scramble with Spinach, Tomatoes, and Feta Cheese

Ingredients:

- 1 block of firm tofu, drained and crumbled
- 1 tablespoon olive oil
- 1/2 onion, chopped
- 2 cloves garlic, minced
- 1/2 teaspoon turmeric
- 1/2 teaspoon paprika
- 1/2 teaspoon cumin
- 1/2 teaspoon salt
- 1/4 teaspoon black pepper
- 2 cups fresh spinach, chopped
- 1/2 cup cherry tomatoes, halved
- 1/4 cup crumbled feta cheese

Instructions:

1. Heat olive oil in a large skillet over medium heat.
2. Add onion and garlic and sauté for 2-3 minutes until softened.
3. Add crumbled tofu, turmeric, paprika, cumin, salt, and black pepper to the skillet and stir to combine.
4. Cook for 5-7 minutes, stirring occasionally, until the tofu is lightly browned and heated through.
5. Add chopped spinach and cherry tomatoes to the skillet and stir to combine.
6. Cook for an additional 2-3 minutes until the spinach is wilted and the tomatoes are heated through.
7. Remove from heat and sprinkle crumbled feta cheese over the top of the scramble.
8. Serve hot and enjoy!

Cooking Time: 15 minutes

Calories per serve (2 people): 300

High-Protein Breakfast Greek Yogurt Parfait with Granola and Mixed Berries

Ingredients:

- 1 cup Greek yogurt
- 1/2 cup granola
- 1/2 cup mixed berries (strawberries, blueberries, raspberries)
- 1 tablespoon honey

Instructions:

1. In a bowl, mix the Greek yogurt and honey until well combined.
2. In two glasses or jars, layer the granola, mixed berries, and Greek yogurt mixture.
3. Repeat the layers until the glasses or jars are full.
4. Top with additional mixed berries and granola, if desired.
5. Serve immediately and enjoy!

Cooking Time: 10 minutes

Calories per serve (2 people): 350

Protein-Packed Breakfast Sweet Potato Hash with Ground Turkey, Kale, and Eggs

Ingredients:

- 1 large sweet potato, peeled and diced
- 1/2 pound ground turkey
- 1/2 onion, diced
- 2 cloves garlic, minced
- 2 cups kale, chopped
- 4 eggs
- 1 tablespoon olive oil
- Salt and pepper to taste

Instructions:

1. Heat olive oil in a large skillet over medium heat.
2. Add sweet potato and onion to the skillet and cook for 10-12 minutes, stirring occasionally, until sweet potato is tender.
3. Add garlic and ground turkey to the skillet and cook for 5-7 minutes, breaking up the turkey with a spatula, until turkey is browned and cooked through.
4. Add kale to the skillet and cook for 2-3 minutes, until kale is wilted.
5. Make four wells in the sweet potato mixture and crack an egg into each well.
6. Cover the skillet and cook for 5-7 minutes, until eggs are cooked to your liking.
7. Season with salt and pepper to taste.
8. Divide the sweet potato hash and eggs between two plates and serve.

Cooking Time: 30 minutes

Calories per serve (2 people): 450

High-Protein Breakfast Banana Bread with Almond Flour and Chocolate Chips

Ingredients:

- 2 ripe bananas, mashed
- 2 eggs
- 1/4 cup honey
- 1/4 cup almond milk
- 1 tsp vanilla extract
- 2 cups almond flour
- 1 tsp baking powder
- 1/2 tsp baking soda
- 1/4 tsp salt
- 1/2 cup dark chocolate chips

Instructions:

1. Preheat the oven to 350°F (180°C). Grease a loaf pan with cooking spray.
2. In a large bowl, whisk together the mashed bananas, eggs, honey, almond milk, and vanilla extract.
3. In a separate bowl, mix together the almond flour, baking powder, baking soda, and salt.
4. Add the dry ingredients to the wet ingredients and stir until well combined.
5. Fold in the chocolate chips.
6. Pour the batter into the prepared loaf pan and smooth out the top with a spatula.
7. Bake for 45-50 minutes, or until a toothpick inserted into the center comes out clean.
8. Let the banana bread cool in the pan for 10 minutes before removing it and slicing it into 8 pieces.

Cooking Time: 50 minutes

Calories per serve (2 people): 350

Protein-Packed Breakfast Quinoa Salad with Roasted Vegetables and Poached Eggs

Ingredients:

- 1 cup quinoa
- 2 cups water
- 1 red bell pepper, sliced
- 1 yellow bell pepper, sliced
- 1 zucchini, sliced
- 1 red onion, sliced
- 2 tablespoons olive oil
- 1 teaspoon salt
- 1/2 teaspoon black pepper
- 4 eggs
- 2 cups baby spinach
- 1/4 cup crumbled feta cheese

Instructions:

1. Preheat the oven to 400°F (200°C).
2. Rinse the quinoa in a fine mesh strainer and add it to a medium saucepan with the water. Bring to a boil, then reduce the heat to low and cover. Cook for 15-20 minutes, or until the water is absorbed and the quinoa is tender.
3. Meanwhile, toss the sliced bell peppers, zucchini, and red onion with the olive oil, salt, and black pepper. Spread the vegetables out on a baking sheet and roast for 20-25 minutes, or until tender and lightly browned.
4. While the vegetables are roasting, poach the eggs. Fill a medium saucepan with water and bring to a simmer. Crack each egg into a small bowl or ramekin. Use a spoon to create a whirlpool in the simmering water, then gently pour the egg into the center of the whirlpool. Cook for 3-4 minutes, or until the whites are set but the yolks are still runny. Use a slotted spoon to remove the eggs from the water and drain on a paper towel.
5. Divide the cooked quinoa between two bowls. Top each bowl with half of the roasted vegetables, 2 poached eggs, and 1 cup of baby spinach. Sprinkle with crumbled feta cheese and serve immediately.

Cooking Time: 45 minutes

Calories per serve (2 people): 480

High-Protein Breakfast Chia Seed Pudding with Almond Milk and Fresh Fruit

Ingredients:

- 1/4 cup chia seeds

- 1 cup unsweetened almond milk

- 1 tablespoon honey

- 1/2 teaspoon vanilla extract

- Fresh fruit (such as berries, sliced banana, or chopped mango) for topping

Instructions:

1. In a medium bowl, whisk together chia seeds, almond milk, honey, and vanilla extract until well combined.

2. Let the mixture sit for 5 minutes, then whisk again to prevent clumps from forming.

3. Cover the bowl with plastic wrap and refrigerate for at least 2 hours or overnight.

4. When ready to serve, divide the chia seed pudding between two bowls or glasses.

5. Top with fresh fruit and enjoy!

Cooking Time: 10 minutes

Calories per serve (2 people): 250

Protein-Packed Breakfast Burrito Bowl with Quinoa, Black Beans, and Avocado

Ingredients:

- 1/2 cup quinoa
- 1 cup water
- 1/2 teaspoon salt
- 1/2 teaspoon ground cumin
- 1/2 teaspoon chili powder
- 1/2 teaspoon garlic powder
- 1/2 cup canned black beans, drained and rinsed
- 1/2 avocado, diced
- 2 eggs
- 1 tablespoon olive oil
- Salt and pepper, to taste

Ingredients:

1. Rinse quinoa in a fine mesh strainer and add to a medium saucepan with water and salt. Bring to a boil, then reduce heat to low and cover. Cook for 15-20 minutes, or until water is absorbed and quinoa is tender.
2. In a small bowl, mix together cumin, chili powder, and garlic powder. Set aside.
3. In a small skillet, heat olive oil over medium heat. Crack eggs into skillet and season with salt and pepper. Cook until whites are set and yolks are still runny, about 2-3 minutes.
4. Divide cooked quinoa between two bowls. Top with black beans, diced avocado, and cooked eggs. Sprinkle with spice mixture and serve.

Cooking Time: 25 minutes

Calories per serve (2 people): 400

High-Protein Breakfast Egg and Cheese Breakfast Sandwich with Grilled Chicken Breast and Spinach

Ingredients:

- 2 whole wheat English muffins
- 2 slices of cheddar cheese
- 2 large eggs
- 1 grilled chicken breast, sliced
- 1 cup of fresh spinach leaves
- 1 tablespoon of olive oil
- Salt and pepper to taste

Ingredients:

1. Preheat a non-stick skillet over medium heat.
2. Split the English muffins in half and toast them in a toaster or under the broiler until lightly browned.
3. Place a slice of cheese on each half of the English muffins.
4. In the same skillet, heat the olive oil over medium heat.
5. Add the spinach leaves and sauté until wilted, about 2-3 minutes.
6. Remove the spinach from the skillet and set aside.
7. In the same skillet, crack the eggs and cook until the whites are set and the yolks are still runny, about 2-3 minutes.
8. Season the eggs with salt and pepper to taste.
9. Assemble the sandwiches by placing the sliced chicken breast on top of the cheese, followed by the sautéed spinach and the fried egg.
10. Top with the other half of the English muffin and serve immediately.

Cooking Time: 15 minutes

Calories per serve (2 people): 450 calories

Protein-Packed Breakfast Cottage Cheese and Veggie Omelette with Bell Peppers, Onions, and Tomatoes

Ingredients:

- 4 eggs
- 1/2 cup cottage cheese
- 1/2 red bell pepper, diced
- 1/2 yellow onion, diced
- 1/2 tomato, diced
- 1 tablespoon olive oil
- Salt and pepper to taste

Ingredients:

1. In a bowl, whisk together the eggs and cottage cheese. Set aside.
2. Heat the olive oil in a non-stick skillet over medium heat.
3. Add the diced bell pepper and onion to the skillet and sauté for 3-4 minutes, until softened.
4. Add the diced tomato to the skillet and sauté for an additional 1-2 minutes.
5. Pour the egg mixture into the skillet and cook for 3-4 minutes, until the bottom is set.
6. Using a spatula, fold the omelette in half and cook for an additional 1-2 minutes, until the eggs are fully cooked.
7. Season with salt and pepper to taste.
8. Serve hot and enjoy!

Cooking Time: 15 minutes

Calories per serve (2 people): 250 calories

High-Protein Breakfast Sweet Potato and Sausage Hash with Poached Eggs

Ingredients:

- 1 large sweet potato, peeled and diced
- 2 tablespoons olive oil
- 1/2 onion, diced
- 2 garlic cloves, minced
- 2 sausages, sliced
- 1/2 teaspoon paprika
- 1/2 teaspoon salt
- 1/4 teaspoon black pepper
- 4 eggs

Instructions:

1. Preheat the oven to 400°F (200°C).
2. In a large bowl, toss the sweet potato with 1 tablespoon of olive oil, paprika, salt, and black pepper.
3. Spread the sweet potato on a baking sheet and bake for 20-25 minutes, or until tender and lightly browned.
4. Meanwhile, heat the remaining 1 tablespoon of olive oil in a large skillet over medium heat.
5. Add the onion and garlic and sauté for 2-3 minutes, or until softened.
6. Add the sliced sausage and cook for 5-7 minutes, or until browned.
7. Add the roasted sweet potato to the skillet and stir to combine.
8. Reduce the heat to low and let the hash cook for another 5-7 minutes, or until heated through.
9. While the hash is cooking, poach the eggs in a separate pot of boiling water for 3-4 minutes, or until the whites are set and the yolks are still runny.
10. Divide the sweet potato and sausage hash between two plates and top each with two poached eggs.
11. Serve immediately.

Cooking Time: 30 minutes

Calories per serve (2 people): 450

Protein-Packed Breakfast Protein Smoothie Bowl with Greek Yogurt, Berries, and Nuts

Ingredients:

- 1 cup frozen mixed berries
- 1 banana
- 1/2 cup plain Greek yogurt
- 1/2 cup unsweetened almond milk
- 1 scoop vanilla protein powder
- 1/4 cup chopped nuts (such as almonds or walnuts)
- 1 tablespoon chia seeds

Instructions:

1. Add the frozen berries, banana, Greek yogurt, almond milk, and protein powder to a blender. Blend until smooth.
2. Pour the smoothie into two bowls.
3. Top each bowl with chopped nuts and chia seeds.
4. Serve immediately.

Cooking Time: 5 minutes

Calories per serve (2 people): 350

High-Protein Breakfast Shakshuka with Eggs, Tomatoes, and Chickpeas

Ingredients:

- 1 tablespoon olive oil
- 1 onion, chopped
- 2 garlic cloves, minced
- 1 red bell pepper, chopped
- 1 can (14.5 ounces) diced tomatoes
- 1 can (15 ounces) chickpeas, drained and rinsed
- 1 teaspoon ground cumin
- 1/2 teaspoon smoked paprika
- 1/4 teaspoon cayenne pepper
- Salt and pepper, to taste
- 4 large eggs
- 2 tablespoons chopped fresh parsley

Instructions:

1. Heat the olive oil in a large skillet over medium heat. Add the onion and garlic and cook until softened, about 5 minutes.
2. Add the red bell pepper and cook for another 5 minutes.
3. Add the diced tomatoes, chickpeas, cumin, smoked paprika, cayenne pepper, salt, and pepper. Stir to combine and bring to a simmer.
4. Use a spoon to make 4 wells in the tomato mixture. Crack an egg into each well.
5. Cover the skillet and cook until the eggs are set, about 5-7 minutes.
6. Sprinkle with chopped parsley and serve hot.

Cooking Time: 25 minutes

Calories per serve (2 people): 400 calories

Protein-Packed Breakfast Grilled Chicken and Veggie Skewers with Yogurt-Dill Sauce

Ingredients:

- 2 boneless, skinless chicken breasts, cut into cubes
- 1 red bell pepper, cut into chunks
- 1 yellow bell pepper, cut into chunks
- 1 zucchini, sliced into rounds
- 1 red onion, cut into chunks
- 1/4 cup olive oil
- 1 teaspoon garlic powder
- 1 teaspoon onion powder
- 1 teaspoon dried oregano
- 1/2 teaspoon salt
- 1/4 teaspoon black pepper
- 1/2 cup plain Greek yogurt
- 1 tablespoon chopped fresh dill
- 1 tablespoon lemon juice

Instructions:

1. Preheat grill to medium-high heat.
2. Thread chicken, bell peppers, zucchini, and red onion onto skewers.
3. In a small bowl, whisk together olive oil, garlic powder, onion powder, oregano, salt, and black pepper.
4. Brush skewers with olive oil mixture.
5. Grill skewers for 10-12 minutes, turning occasionally, until chicken is cooked through and vegetables are tender.
6. In another small bowl, whisk together Greek yogurt, dill, and lemon juice.
7. Serve skewers with yogurt-dill sauce.

Cooking Time: 20 minutes

Calories per serve (2 people): 350

High-Protein Breakfast Veggie Quinoa Breakfast Bowl with Tofu and Cashews

Ingredients:

- 1/2 cup quinoa
- 1 cup water
- 1/2 block of firm tofu, drained and cubed
- 1/2 red bell pepper, sliced
- 1/2 yellow bell pepper, sliced
- 1/2 onion, sliced
- 1/2 cup cashews
- 1 tablespoon olive oil
- 1/2 teaspoon garlic powder
- 1/2 teaspoon onion powder
- Salt and pepper to taste

Instructions:

1. Rinse quinoa in a fine mesh strainer and add to a medium saucepan with water. Bring to a boil, then reduce heat to low and cover. Cook for 15-20 minutes or until water is absorbed and quinoa is tender.
2. While quinoa is cooking, heat olive oil in a large skillet over medium-high heat. Add tofu and cook for 5-7 minutes or until lightly browned. Remove from skillet and set aside.
3. Add sliced bell peppers and onion to the same skillet and cook for 5-7 minutes or until tender. Add garlic powder, onion powder, salt, and pepper to taste.
4. Divide cooked quinoa between two bowls. Top with cooked tofu, sautéed veggies, and cashews.
5. Serve and enjoy!

Cooking Time: 30 minutes

Calories per serve (2 people): 450

Protein-Packed Breakfast Huevos Rancheros with Black Beans, Avocado, and Salsa

Ingredients:

- 4 corn tortillas
- 1 can black beans, drained and rinsed
- 1 avocado, sliced
- 1/2 cup salsa
- 4 eggs
- 1/4 cup shredded cheddar cheese
- 1 tablespoon olive oil
- Salt and pepper to taste

Instructions:

1. Preheat oven to 350°F.
2. Heat olive oil in a large skillet over medium heat.
3. Add black beans and cook for 5 minutes, stirring occasionally.
4. Place tortillas on a baking sheet and bake for 5 minutes.
5. Crack eggs into the skillet with the black beans and cook until desired doneness.
6. Place tortillas on plates and top each with black beans, an egg, avocado slices, salsa, and shredded cheese.
7. Serve immediately.

Cooking Time: 20 minutes

Calories per serve (2 people): 450

High-Protein Breakfast Blueberry and Quinoa Breakfast Bowl with Almonds and Greek Yogurt

Ingredients:

- 1/2 cup quinoa
- 1 cup water
- 1/2 cup blueberries
- 1/4 cup sliced almonds
- 1/2 cup Greek yogurt
- 1 tablespoon honey

Instructions:

1. Rinse the quinoa in a fine mesh strainer and add it to a medium saucepan with the water. Bring to a boil, then reduce the heat to low and cover. Cook for 15 minutes, or until the water is absorbed and the quinoa is tender.
2. Divide the cooked quinoa between two bowls.
3. Top each bowl with blueberries and sliced almonds.
4. In a small bowl, mix together the Greek yogurt and honey. Spoon the mixture over the top of each bowl.
5. Serve immediately.

Cooking Time: 20 minutes

Calories per serve (2 people): 400

Protein-Packed Breakfast Turkey Bacon and Cheese Frittata with Spinach and Tomatoes

Ingredients:

- 4 slices of turkey bacon, chopped
- 1/2 cup of chopped spinach
- 1/2 cup of chopped tomatoes
- 4 eggs
- 1/4 cup of milk
- 1/4 cup of shredded cheddar cheese
- Salt and pepper to taste

Instructions:

1. Preheat the oven to 375°F (190°C).
2. In a large oven-safe skillet, cook the turkey bacon over medium heat until crispy. Remove from the skillet and set aside.
3. Add the chopped spinach and tomatoes to the skillet and cook until the spinach is wilted and the tomatoes are softened.
4. In a bowl, whisk together the eggs, milk, salt, and pepper.
5. Pour the egg mixture into the skillet and stir to combine with the spinach and tomatoes.
6. Sprinkle the cooked turkey bacon and shredded cheddar cheese over the top of the egg mixture.
7. Transfer the skillet to the preheated oven and bake for 15-20 minutes, or until the eggs are set and the cheese is melted and bubbly.
8. Remove from the oven and let cool for a few minutes before slicing and serving.

Cooking Time: 25 minutes

Calories per serve (2 people): 350

High-Protein Breakfast Protein Waffles with Banana and Peanut Butter

Ingredients:

- 1 cup of whole wheat flour
- 1 scoop of vanilla protein powder
- 1 tablespoon of baking powder
- 1/4 teaspoon of salt
- 1 cup of unsweetened almond milk
- 1 egg
- 1 tablespoon of honey
- 1 banana, sliced
- 2 tablespoons of peanut butter

Instructions:

1. In a large mixing bowl, combine the whole wheat flour, vanilla protein powder, baking powder, and salt.
2. In a separate bowl, whisk together the almond milk, egg, and honey.
3. Pour the wet ingredients into the dry ingredients and mix until well combined.
4. Preheat a waffle iron and spray with cooking spray.
5. Spoon the batter onto the waffle iron and cook until golden brown.
6. Top the waffles with sliced banana and peanut butter.
7. Serve and enjoy!

Cooking Time: 15 minutes

Calories per serve (2 people): 450

Protein-Packed Breakfast Salmon and Avocado Toast with Poached Egg

Ingredients:

- 2 slices of whole grain bread
- 1 avocado, mashed
- 1/2 lemon, juiced
- 1/2 teaspoon garlic powder
- 1/4 teaspoon salt
- 1/4 teaspoon black pepper
- 4 ounces smoked salmon
- 2 eggs
- 1 tablespoon white vinegar

Instructions:

1. Toast the bread slices in a toaster or on a grill until crispy.
2. In a small bowl, mix together the mashed avocado, lemon juice, garlic powder, salt, and black pepper.
3. Spread the avocado mixture evenly on each slice of toast.
4. Top each slice of toast with 2 ounces of smoked salmon.
5. Fill a medium-sized pot with water and bring to a boil. Add the white vinegar to the water.
6. Crack each egg into a small bowl or ramekin.
7. Reduce the heat of the water to a simmer and gently pour each egg into the water. Cook for 3-4 minutes or until the egg whites are set but the yolks are still runny.
8. Remove the poached eggs from the water with a slotted spoon and place one egg on top of each slice of toast.
9. Serve immediately.

Cooking Time: 15 minutes

Calories per serve (2 people): 450 calories

High-Protein Breakfast Sausage and Sweet Potato Breakfast Bowl with Fried Egg

Ingredients:

- 2 sweet potatoes, peeled and cubed
- 2 tablespoons olive oil
- 1/2 teaspoon garlic powder
- 1/2 teaspoon paprika
- 1/2 teaspoon salt
- 1/4 teaspoon black pepper
- 4 breakfast sausages, sliced
- 2 eggs

Instructions:

1. Preheat the oven to 400°F (200°C).
2. In a large bowl, toss the sweet potatoes with olive oil, garlic powder, paprika, salt, and black pepper.
3. Spread the sweet potatoes in a single layer on a baking sheet and bake for 20-25 minutes, or until tender and lightly browned.
4. While the sweet potatoes are cooking, heat a skillet over medium-high heat and cook the breakfast sausage until browned and cooked through, about 5-7 minutes.
5. Remove the sweet potatoes from the oven and divide them between two bowls.
6. Top the sweet potatoes with the cooked breakfast sausage.
7. In the same skillet used to cook the sausage, crack the eggs and fry until the whites are set and the yolks are still runny, about 2-3 minutes.
8. Place one fried egg on top of each bowl and serve immediately.

Cooking Time: 30-35 minutes

Calories per serve (2 people): 550 calories

Protein-Packed Breakfast Breakfast Tacos with Scrambled Eggs, Black Beans, and Salsa

Ingredients:

- 4 corn tortillas
- 4 large eggs
- 1/2 cup canned black beans, drained and rinsed
- 1/4 cup salsa
- 1/4 cup shredded cheddar cheese
- 1 tablespoon olive oil
- Salt and pepper to taste

Instructions:

1. Heat the olive oil in a large skillet over medium heat.
2. Add the black beans and cook for 2-3 minutes, stirring occasionally.
3. Crack the eggs into a bowl and whisk until well beaten.
4. Add the eggs to the skillet with the black beans and cook, stirring occasionally, until the eggs are scrambled and cooked through.
5. Warm the tortillas in the microwave or on a skillet.
6. Divide the scrambled eggs and black beans among the tortillas.
7. Top each taco with salsa and shredded cheese.
8. Season with salt and pepper to taste.
9. Serve immediately.

Cooking Time: 15 minutes

Calories per serve (2 tacos): 400

High-Protein Breakfast Broiled Grapefruit with Yogurt and Almonds

Ingredients:

- 1 large grapefruit, halved
- 2 tablespoons honey
- 1/4 teaspoon ground cinnamon
- 1/2 cup plain Greek yogurt
- 2 tablespoons sliced almonds

Instructions:

1. Preheat the broiler to high.
2. Cut the grapefruit in half and use a knife to loosen the segments from the membrane.
3. In a small bowl, mix together the honey and cinnamon.
4. Brush the honey mixture over the grapefruit halves.
5. Place the grapefruit halves on a baking sheet and broil for 3-5 minutes, or until the tops are golden brown and caramelized.
6. Remove the grapefruit from the oven and let cool for a few minutes.
7. Top each grapefruit half with 1/4 cup of Greek yogurt and 1 tablespoon of sliced almonds.
8. Serve immediately.

Cooking Time: 10 minutes

Calories per serve (2 people): 190

Protein-Packed Breakfast Egg and Cheese Breakfast Quesadilla with Turkey Sausage and Peppers

Ingredients:

- 4 large eggs
- 1/4 cup milk
- 1/4 teaspoon salt
- 1/4 teaspoon black pepper
- 1/2 cup shredded cheddar cheese
- 2 whole wheat tortillas
- 4 turkey sausage links, cooked and sliced
- 1/2 red bell pepper, sliced
- 1/2 green bell pepper, sliced
- 1 tablespoon olive oil

Instructions:

1. In a medium bowl, whisk together the eggs, milk, salt, and black pepper.
2. Heat a large nonstick skillet over medium heat. Add the egg mixture and cook, stirring occasionally, until scrambled and set, about 3-4 minutes. Remove from the skillet and set aside.
3. Wipe out the skillet and return it to medium heat. Add the olive oil and bell peppers and cook, stirring occasionally, until softened, about 3-4 minutes. Remove from the skillet and set aside.
4. Place one tortilla in the skillet over medium heat. Sprinkle half of the cheese over the tortilla. Top with half of the scrambled eggs, half of the turkey sausage, and half of the bell peppers. Sprinkle the remaining cheese over the top. Place the second tortilla on top.
5. Cook until the bottom tortilla is golden brown, about 2-3 minutes. Carefully flip the quesadilla and cook until the second tortilla is golden brown and the cheese is melted, about 2-3 minutes more.
6. Remove from the skillet and cut into wedges. Serve hot.

Cooking Time: 20 minutes

Calories per serve (2 people): 450

High-Protein Breakfast Steak and Egg Breakfast Skillet with Mushrooms and Onions

Ingredients:

- 2 sirloin steaks (4 oz each)
- 1 tablespoon olive oil
- 1/2 onion, sliced
- 1 cup sliced mushrooms
- 4 eggs
- Salt and pepper to taste

Instructions:

1. Heat a large skillet over medium-high heat. Add the olive oil and swirl to coat the pan.
2. Add the steaks to the skillet and cook for 3-4 minutes per side, or until browned and cooked to your desired level of doneness. Remove the steaks from the skillet and set aside.
3. Add the onions and mushrooms to the skillet and cook for 3-4 minutes, or until softened.
4. Crack the eggs into the skillet and cook until the whites are set but the yolks are still runny.
5. Season the steaks, vegetables, and eggs with salt and pepper to taste.
6. Divide the steak, vegetables, and eggs between two plates and serve immediately.

Cooking Time: 20 minutes

Calories per serve (2 people): 400

Protein-Packed Breakfast Peanut Butter Banana Protein Smoothie with Greek Yogurt and Honey

Ingredients:

- 1 ripe banana
- 1 cup Greek yogurt
- 1/2 cup unsweetened almond milk
- 2 tablespoons peanut butter
- 1 scoop vanilla protein powder
- 1 tablespoon honey
- 1/2 teaspoon vanilla extract
- 1 cup ice cubes

Instructions:

1. Peel the banana and place it in a blender.
2. Add the Greek yogurt, almond milk, peanut butter, protein powder, honey, vanilla extract, and ice cubes to the blender.
3. Blend all the ingredients until smooth and creamy.
4. Pour the smoothie into two glasses and serve immediately.

Cooking Time: 5 minutes

Calories per serve (2 people): 350

High-Protein Breakfast Egg and Cheese Breakfast Sandwich with Turkey Bacon and Tomato

Ingredients:

- 4 slices of turkey bacon
- 4 eggs
- 4 slices of whole wheat bread
- 2 slices of cheddar cheese
- 1 tomato, sliced
- Salt and pepper to taste

Instructions:

1. Cook the turkey bacon in a non-stick pan over medium heat until crispy. Remove from pan and set aside.
2. In the same pan, crack the eggs and cook to your desired doneness. Season with salt and pepper to taste.
3. Toast the slices of whole wheat bread.
4. Place a slice of cheddar cheese on two of the slices of toast.
5. Top each slice of cheese toast with two slices of turkey bacon, one cooked egg, and a few slices of tomato.
6. Top with the remaining slices of toast to make two sandwiches.
7. Serve hot and enjoy!

Cooking Time: 10 minutes

Calories per serve (2 people): 450

Protein-Packed Breakfast Spinach and Feta Breakfast Wrap with Egg Whites

Ingredients:

- 4 egg whites
- 1/4 cup crumbled feta cheese
- 1/2 cup fresh spinach leaves
- 2 whole wheat tortillas
- 1/4 teaspoon salt
- 1/4 teaspoon black pepper
- 1 tablespoon olive oil

Instructions:

1. In a small bowl, whisk together the egg whites, salt, and black pepper.
2. Heat the olive oil in a non-stick skillet over medium heat.
3. Add the egg white mixture to the skillet and cook, stirring occasionally, until the eggs are set, about 3-4 minutes.
4. Divide the spinach leaves between the two tortillas, placing them in the center of each tortilla.
5. Top the spinach with the scrambled egg whites and crumbled feta cheese.
6. Roll up the tortillas, tucking in the sides as you go.
7. Place the wraps seam-side down in the skillet and cook for 1-2 minutes on each side, until the tortillas are lightly browned and crispy.
8. Serve immediately.

Cooking Time: 15 minutes

Calories per serve (2 people): 280 calories

High-Protein Breakfast Greek Yogurt Parfait with Berries, Granola, and Honey

Ingredients:

- 1 cup Greek yogurt
- 1/2 cup mixed berries (such as strawberries, blueberries, and raspberries)
- 1/4 cup granola
- 1 tablespoon honey

Instructions:

1. Divide the Greek yogurt evenly between two serving glasses or bowls.
2. Top each serving with half of the mixed berries.
3. Sprinkle 2 tablespoons of granola over each serving.
4. Drizzle 1/2 tablespoon of honey over each serving.
5. Enjoy immediately or refrigerate until ready to serve.

Cooking Time: 5 minutes

Calories per serve (2 people): 250

Protein-Packed Breakfast Broccoli and Cheddar Breakfast Casserole with Turkey Sausage

Ingredients:

- 1 tablespoon olive oil
- 1/2 pound turkey sausage, casings removed
- 1 small onion, chopped
- 2 cups chopped broccoli florets
- 6 large eggs
- 1/2 cup milk
- 1/2 teaspoon salt
- 1/4 teaspoon black pepper
- 1 cup shredded cheddar cheese

Instructions:

1. Preheat oven to 375°F. Grease an 8-inch square baking dish with cooking spray.
2. In a large skillet, heat olive oil over medium heat. Add turkey sausage and cook, breaking up with a spoon, until browned and cooked through, about 5 minutes.
3. Add onion and broccoli to the skillet and cook until vegetables are tender, about 5 minutes.
4. In a large bowl, whisk together eggs, milk, salt, and pepper. Stir in cooked sausage and vegetables.
5. Pour egg mixture into prepared baking dish. Sprinkle shredded cheddar cheese on top.
6. Bake for 25-30 minutes, or until eggs are set and cheese is melted and bubbly.
7. Let cool for a few minutes before slicing and serving.

Cooking Time: 35-40 minutes

Calories per serve (2 people): 450

High-Protein Breakfast Steak and Egg Breakfast Burrito with Black Beans and Avocado

Ingredients:

- 2 flour tortillas
- 1/2 pound flank steak, sliced into thin strips
- 4 eggs
- 1/2 cup black beans, drained and rinsed
- 1 avocado, sliced
- 1/4 cup shredded cheddar cheese
- 1 tablespoon olive oil
- Salt and pepper to taste

Instructions:

1. Heat the olive oil in a large skillet over medium-high heat.
2. Add the sliced flank steak and cook for 3-4 minutes, or until browned on all sides.
3. Remove the steak from the skillet and set aside.
4. In the same skillet, crack the eggs and cook to your desired doneness.
5. Warm the tortillas in the microwave or on a skillet.
6. Divide the steak, eggs, black beans, avocado, and shredded cheese between the two tortillas.
7. Season with salt and pepper to taste.
8. Roll up the tortillas and serve immediately.

Cooking Time: 20 minutes

Calories per serve (2 people): 550

Protein-Packed Breakfast Oatmeal with Peanut Butter and Banana

Ingredients:

- 1 cup rolled oats
- 2 cups water
- 1/4 cup peanut butter
- 1 banana, sliced
- 1 scoop vanilla protein powder
- 1 tablespoon honey

Instructions:

1. In a medium saucepan, bring the water to a boil.
2. Add the rolled oats and reduce the heat to low. Cook for 5-7 minutes, stirring occasionally, until the oats are tender and the mixture has thickened.
3. Remove the saucepan from the heat and stir in the peanut butter, banana slices, protein powder, and honey until well combined.
4. Divide the oatmeal between two bowls and serve immediately.

Cooking Time: 10 minutes

Calories per serve: 450

High-Protein Breakfast Smoked Salmon and Cream Cheese Bagel with Capers and Red Onion

Ingredients:

- 2 bagels, sliced in half
- 4 oz smoked salmon
- 4 oz cream cheese
- 2 tbsp capers
- 1/4 red onion, thinly sliced

Instructions:

1. Toast the bagels until lightly browned.
2. Spread the cream cheese on each half of the bagel.
3. Top each half with smoked salmon.
4. Sprinkle capers and red onion on top of the smoked salmon.
5. Serve and enjoy!

Cooking Time: 10 minutes

Calories per serve (2 people): 450 calories

Protein-Packed Breakfast Veggie and Egg Scramble with Mushrooms, Tomatoes, and Onions

Ingredients:

- 4 eggs
- 1/2 cup sliced mushrooms
- 1/2 cup diced tomatoes
- 1/4 cup diced onions
- 1 tablespoon olive oil
- Salt and pepper to taste

Instructions:

1. Heat the olive oil in a non-stick skillet over medium heat.
2. Add the onions and cook until they are translucent, about 2-3 minutes.
3. Add the mushrooms and cook until they are tender, about 3-4 minutes.
4. Add the tomatoes and cook until they are heated through, about 1-2 minutes.
5. In a separate bowl, whisk the eggs together with salt and pepper.
6. Pour the eggs into the skillet with the vegetables and stir until the eggs are cooked through, about 3-4 minutes.
7. Divide the scramble into two plates and serve hot.

Cooking Time: 15 minutes

Calories per serve (2 people): 250

High-Protein Breakfast Bacon and Cheddar Breakfast Muffins with Almond Flour

Ingredients:

- 6 slices of bacon, cooked and crumbled
- 1 cup almond flour
- 1/2 cup shredded cheddar cheese
- 1/4 cup chopped green onions
- 1/4 cup unsweetened almond milk
- 2 large eggs
- 1/2 teaspoon baking powder
- 1/4 teaspoon salt

Instructions:

1. Preheat the oven to 350°F (175°C). Grease a muffin tin with cooking spray or line with muffin cups.
2. In a large mixing bowl, whisk together the almond flour, baking powder, and salt.
3. In a separate bowl, beat the eggs and almond milk together. Add the crumbled bacon, shredded cheddar cheese, and chopped green onions to the egg mixture and stir to combine.
4. Pour the egg mixture into the almond flour mixture and stir until well combined.
5. Spoon the batter into the muffin cups, filling each about 3/4 full.
6. Bake for 20-25 minutes, or until the muffins are golden brown and a toothpick inserted into the center comes out clean.
7. Allow the muffins to cool for a few minutes before removing them from the muffin tin. Serve warm.

Cooking Time: 20-25 minutes

Calories per serve (2 muffins): 420

Protein-Packed Breakfast Chocolate Protein Pancakes with Greek Yogurt and Berries

Ingredients:

- 1/2 cup rolled oats
- 1/2 cup cottage cheese
- 1/2 cup egg whites
- 1 scoop chocolate protein powder
- 1/2 tsp baking powder
- 1/4 tsp vanilla extract
- 1/4 cup Greek yogurt
- 1/2 cup mixed berries

Instructions:

1. In a blender, combine rolled oats, cottage cheese, egg whites, chocolate protein powder, baking powder, and vanilla extract. Blend until smooth.
2. Heat a non-stick pan over medium heat. Pour 1/4 cup of the batter onto the pan and cook until bubbles form on the surface, then flip and cook for another 1-2 minutes. Repeat with remaining batter.
3. Top each pancake with Greek yogurt and mixed berries.
4. Serve and enjoy!

Cooking Time: 15 minutes

Calories per serve (2 pancakes): 350

High-Protein Breakfast Banana and Peanut Butter Protein Smoothie with Greek Yogurt and Chocolate Chips

Ingredients:

- 1 ripe banana
- 2 tablespoons peanut butter
- 1/2 cup Greek yogurt
- 1/2 cup unsweetened almond milk
- 1 scoop vanilla protein powder
- 1 tablespoon chocolate chips

Instructions:

1. Peel the banana and place it in a blender.
2. Add the peanut butter, Greek yogurt, almond milk, and protein powder to the blender.
3. Blend all the ingredients until smooth.
4. Pour the smoothie into two glasses.
5. Sprinkle the chocolate chips on top of the smoothie.
6. Enjoy your High-Protein Breakfast Banana and Peanut Butter Protein Smoothie with Greek Yogurt and Chocolate Chips!

Cooking Time: 5 minutes

Calories per serve (2 people): 350

Protein-Packed Breakfast Chicken and Egg Breakfast Bowl with Quinoa and Avocado

Ingredients:

- 1/2 cup quinoa
- 1 cup water
- 1/2 avocado, sliced
- 1/2 cup cherry tomatoes, halved
- 1/4 cup red onion, diced
- 1/4 cup fresh cilantro, chopped
- 1 tablespoon olive oil
- 2 boneless, skinless chicken breasts
- 1/2 teaspoon garlic powder
- 1/2 teaspoon paprika
- 1/2 teaspoon salt
- 1/4 teaspoon black pepper
- 4 eggs

Instructions:

1. Rinse quinoa in a fine mesh strainer and add to a medium saucepan with water. Bring to a boil, then reduce heat to low and cover. Cook for 15-20 minutes, or until water is absorbed and quinoa is tender.
2. In a large bowl, combine cooked quinoa, avocado, cherry tomatoes, red onion, and cilantro. Toss with olive oil and set aside.
3. Season chicken breasts with garlic powder, paprika, salt, and black pepper. Heat a large skillet over medium-high heat and add chicken. Cook for 5-7 minutes per side, or until cooked through. Remove from skillet and let rest for 5 minutes before slicing.
4. In the same skillet, crack eggs and cook to desired doneness.
5. To assemble bowls, divide quinoa mixture between two bowls. Top with sliced chicken and a cooked egg. Serve immediately.

Cooking Time: 30 minutes

Calories per serve (2 people): 550

High-Protein Breakfast Cottage Cheese and Tomato Breakfast Toast with Sprouts and Balsamic Glaze

Ingredients:

- 2 slices of whole grain bread
- 1/2 cup of cottage cheese
- 1 tomato, sliced
- 1/4 cup of sprouts
- 1 tablespoon of balsamic glaze
- Salt and pepper to taste

Instructions:

1. Toast the bread slices until golden brown.
2. Spread the cottage cheese evenly on each slice of toast.
3. Top each slice with sliced tomatoes.
4. Sprinkle salt and pepper over the tomatoes.
5. Add sprouts on top of the tomatoes.
6. Drizzle balsamic glaze over the sprouts.
7. Serve immediately.

Cooking Time: 10 minutes

Calories per serve (2 people): 250 calories

Protein-Packed Breakfast Huevos Rancheros Breakfast Skillet with Black Beans and Cheddar Cheese

Ingredients:

- 1 tablespoon olive oil
- 1/2 onion, diced
- 1/2 red bell pepper, diced
- 1 garlic clove, minced
- 1/2 teaspoon ground cumin
- 1/2 teaspoon chili powder
- 1/2 teaspoon paprika
- 1/2 teaspoon salt
- 1/4 teaspoon black pepper
- 1 can (15 ounces) black beans, drained and rinsed
- 4 large eggs
- 1/2 cup shredded cheddar cheese
- 1/4 cup chopped fresh cilantro

Instructions:

1. Preheat oven to 375°F.
2. In a large oven-safe skillet, heat olive oil over medium heat. Add onion and red bell pepper and cook until softened, about 5 minutes.
3. Add garlic, cumin, chili powder, paprika, salt, and black pepper and cook for 1 minute.
4. Add black beans and cook until heated through, about 2 minutes.
5. Make 4 wells in the bean mixture and crack an egg into each well.
6. Sprinkle cheddar cheese over the top of the skillet and transfer to the oven.
7. Bake until the egg whites are set and the yolks are still runny, about 10-12 minutes.
8. Sprinkle with cilantro and serve hot.

Cooking Time: 25 minutes

Calories per serve (2 people): 450

High-Protein Breakfast Egg White and Spinach Breakfast Sandwich with Turkey Sausage and Pepper Jack Cheese

Ingredients:

- 4 egg whites
- 1/2 cup fresh spinach, chopped
- 2 turkey sausage patties
- 2 slices pepper jack cheese
- 2 whole wheat English muffins, split and toasted
- Salt and pepper, to taste

Instructions:

1. Cook the turkey sausage patties according to package instructions.
2. In a small bowl, whisk together the egg whites, chopped spinach, salt, and pepper.
3. Heat a non-stick skillet over medium heat. Pour the egg white mixture into the skillet and cook until set, about 3-4 minutes.
4. Place a slice of pepper jack cheese on top of the cooked egg white and let it melt slightly.
5. Place the cooked turkey sausage patty on one half of the toasted English muffin. Top with the egg white and spinach mixture and the other half of the English muffin.
6. Serve immediately.

Cooking Time: 10 minutes

Calories per serve (2 people): 350 calories

Protein-Packed Breakfast Turkey and Egg Breakfast Casserole with Sweet Potato and Green Beans

Ingredients:

- 1 large sweet potato, peeled and diced
- 1/2 pound ground turkey
- 1/2 cup diced onion
- 1/2 cup diced green bell pepper
- 1/2 cup diced red bell pepper
- 1 cup green beans, trimmed and cut into 1-inch pieces
- 4 large eggs
- 1/4 cup milk
- 1/2 teaspoon salt
- 1/4 teaspoon black pepper
- 1/4 teaspoon garlic powder
- 1/4 teaspoon onion powder
- 1/4 teaspoon dried thyme
- 1/4 teaspoon dried oregano
- 1/4 teaspoon paprika

Instructions:

1. Preheat oven to 375°F.
2. Place sweet potato in a large pot of boiling water and cook for 5 minutes. Drain and set aside.
3. In a large skillet, cook ground turkey over medium heat until browned. Add onion, green bell pepper, and red bell pepper and cook until vegetables are tender, about 5 minutes.
4. Add green beans and sweet potato to the skillet and cook for an additional 5 minutes.
5. In a separate bowl, whisk together eggs, milk, salt, black pepper, garlic powder, onion powder, dried thyme, dried oregano, and paprika.
6. Grease a 9x9 inch baking dish and pour the turkey and vegetable mixture into the dish. Pour the egg mixture over the top.
7. Bake for 25-30 minutes or until the eggs are set and the top is golden brown.

8. Serve hot and enjoy!

Cooking Time: 45 minutes

Calories per serve (2 people): 350

High-Protein Breakfast Quinoa and Egg Breakfast Bowl with Kale, Sweet Potato, and Feta Cheese

Ingredients:

- 1/2 cup quinoa
- 1 cup water
- 1/2 sweet potato, peeled and diced
- 1 tablespoon olive oil
- 2 cups kale, chopped
- 4 eggs
- 1/4 cup crumbled feta cheese
- Salt and pepper to taste

Instructions:

1. Rinse quinoa in a fine mesh strainer and add to a medium saucepan with water. Bring to a boil, then reduce heat to low and cover. Cook for 15-20 minutes or until water is absorbed and quinoa is tender.
2. While quinoa is cooking, heat olive oil in a large skillet over medium heat. Add sweet potato and cook for 5-7 minutes or until tender.
3. Add kale to the skillet and cook for an additional 2-3 minutes or until wilted.
4. In a separate skillet, cook eggs to your desired doneness.
5. Divide quinoa between two bowls. Top with sweet potato and kale mixture, then add eggs on top. Sprinkle with feta cheese and season with salt and pepper to taste.
6. Serve immediately.

Cooking Time: 30 minutes

Calories per serve (2 people): 450

Protein-Packed Breakfast Ham and Cheese Breakfast Muffins with Almond Flour and Broccoli

Ingredients:

- 1 cup almond flour
- 1/2 teaspoon baking powder
- 1/4 teaspoon salt
- 1/4 teaspoon black pepper
- 1/2 cup chopped broccoli
- 1/2 cup diced ham
- 1/2 cup shredded cheddar cheese
- 2 large eggs
- 1/4 cup unsweetened almond milk

Instructions:

1. Preheat the oven to 375°F (190°C). Grease a muffin tin with cooking spray.
2. In a large bowl, whisk together the almond flour, baking powder, salt, and black pepper.
3. Add the chopped broccoli, diced ham, and shredded cheddar cheese to the bowl and stir to combine.
4. In a separate bowl, whisk together the eggs and almond milk.
5. Pour the egg mixture into the bowl with the dry ingredients and stir until well combined.
6. Spoon the mixture evenly into the muffin tin, filling each cup about 3/4 full.
7. Bake for 20-25 minutes, or until the muffins are golden brown and a toothpick inserted into the center comes out clean.
8. Remove the muffins from the oven and let cool for a few minutes before serving.

Cooking Time: 25 minutes

Calories per serve (2 people): 350

High-Protein Breakfast Greek Yogurt and Berry Breakfast Smoothie Bowl with Almonds and Chia Seeds

Ingredients:

- 1 cup Greek yogurt
- 1 cup frozen mixed berries
- 1 banana
- 1/4 cup almond milk
- 1/4 cup sliced almonds
- 2 tablespoons chia seeds

Instructions:

1. In a blender, combine the Greek yogurt, frozen mixed berries, banana, and almond milk. Blend until smooth.
2. Pour the smoothie into two bowls.
3. Sprinkle sliced almonds and chia seeds on top of each bowl.
4. Serve immediately.

Cooking Time: 5 minutes

Calories per serve (2 people): 350

Protein-Packed Breakfast Mushroom and Cheese Omelette with Egg Whites and Spinach

Ingredients:

- 4 egg whites
- 1/2 cup sliced mushrooms
- 1/4 cup shredded cheddar cheese
- 1/2 cup fresh spinach leaves
- 1 tablespoon olive oil
- Salt and pepper to taste

Instructions:

1. In a small bowl, whisk the egg whites with salt and pepper until frothy.
2. Heat the olive oil in a non-stick skillet over medium heat.
3. Add the mushrooms and sauté for 2-3 minutes until tender.
4. Add the spinach leaves and sauté for another minute until wilted.
5. Pour the egg whites into the skillet and let cook for 2-3 minutes until set.
6. Sprinkle the shredded cheese on top of the omelette and fold it in half.
7. Cook for another minute until the cheese is melted and the omelette is golden brown.
8. Slide the omelette onto a plate and serve hot.

Cooking Time: 10 minutes

Calories per serve (2 people): 200 calories

Made in United States
North Haven, CT
26 January 2024

47740182R00063